How to Be a Scientist

Watch Out!
Science Tools and Safety

Susan Glass

Heinemann Library
Chicago, Illinois

Customer Service 888–454–2279

Visit our website at www.hcinemannllbrary.com

Photo research by Ruth Blair and Ginny Stroud-Lewis
Designed by Victoria Bevan, Ron Kamen and AMR Design Ltd
Printed in China by WKT Company Ltd

11 10 09 08 07
10 9 8 7 6 5 4 3 2 1

Library of Congress Cataloging-in-Publication Data
Glass, Susan.
 Watch out! : science tools and safety / Susan Glass.
   p. cm. -- (How to be a scientist)
 Includes bibliographical references and index.
 ISBN-13: 978-1-4034-8360-7 (library binding (hardcover))
 ISBN-10: 1-4034-8360-4 (library binding (hardcover))
 ISBN-13: 978-1-4034-8364-5 (pbk.)
 ISBN-10: 1-4034-8364-7 (pbk.)
 1. Scientific apparatus and instruments--Juvenile literature. 2. Science--Measurement--
Juvenile literature.
 3. Science--Experiments--Safety measures--Juvenile literature. I. Title. II. Series: Glass,
Susan. How to be a scientist.
 Q185.3.G57 2006
 502.8--dc22
                        2006010840

Acknowledgments
The author and publisher are grateful to the following for permission to reproduce copyright
material: Alamy Images p. 26, Alamy Images pp. 36 (ACE STOCK LIMITED), 7 (Leslie Garland
Picture Library), 33 (ImageState); ;Corbis pp. 8, 11, 38; Corbis pp. 34 (Anthony Redpath), 16
(Austrian Archives), 4 (Bettmann), 13 (JLP/Jose Luis Pelaez/zefa), 31 (Lawrence Manning), 28
(Roger Ressmeyer); Getty Images/Photodisc pp. 6, 18, 25, 32, 40, 41; Ginny Stroud-Lewis p.
23; Harcourt Education/Tudor Photography pp. 14, 15, 29, 35, 37, 39; Jupiter Images p. 21;
Mary Evans Picture Library pp. 22, 24; NASA pp. 20, 30, Science Photo Library pp. 5 (COLIN
CUTHBERT), 43 (CAMR / A.B. DOWSETT), 9 (DOUGLAS FAULKNER), 42 (DAVID PARKER), 19
(CRISTINA PEDRAZZINI).

Cover photograph of laboratory glassware reproduced with permission of Science Photo
Library/Tek Image

The publishers would like to thank Bronwen Howells for her assistance in the preparation of
this book.

Every effort has been made to contact copyright holders of any material reproduced in
this book. Any omissions will be rectified in subsequent printings if notice is given to the
publisher.

Dedication
I would like to thank my husband, John, for all his help and encouragement. I want to
dedicate this book to him, my parents, my children Joanna, John, Billy, and Tricia, and my
granddaughter Madison.

Contents

Some words are shown in bold, **like this**. You can find out what they mean by looking in the glossary.

Science Tools

Anton van Leeuwenhoek (pronounced "lay-ven-hook") lived in the Dutch city of Delft in the 1600–1700s. He did not have a science education, but he did have a talent for careful **observation**. He also had one of the most important tools of science—a **microscope**. Van Leeuwenhoek did not invent the microscope. But he made microscopes far more powerful than they were before. He created **lenses** that could make things look up to 300 times larger.

Using a microscope, van Leeuwenhoek discovered what he called "animalcules," or tiny animals, swimming in water. He was the first person ever to see microscopic living things.

Today we call them microorganisms, or microbes. Van Leeuwenhoek also discovered **bacteria**. With this new tool of science, the microscope, van Leeuwenhoek discovered whole new worlds.

Anton van Leeuwenhoek was the first person to use very powerful microscopes.

This scientist is using a scanning electron microscope, which is much more powerful than van Leeuwenhoek's.

The scientific method

Van Leeuwenhoek was not a professional scientist. But just like a scientist, he investigated the world in an orderly way. Scientists all over the world use the **scientific method**. Using this method, scientists:

1. Ask questions about the world and make observations. Tools such as microscopes can help them observe.
2. Form a **hypothesis**, or what they think is the answer to a question. The hypothesis is a statement they can test.
3. Plan an experiment to find the answer.
4. Conduct the experiment, taking careful notes.
5. Draw conclusions based on the results. Then they share what they learned with other scientists.

Scientists make use of many different tools as they follow the scientific method. You should learn how to use them if you want to know how to be a scientist.

TOP TIP

Some scientists do dangerous work. They deal with germs, animals, dangerous chemicals, or even hot lava. Part of planning a good experiment is planning for safety. Real scientists are aware of safety and students should be too. Safety comes first! Turn to pages 40–41 for important safety advice.

Observation

A tool is something that is used to help complete a task. Not all tools are things you can touch and hold. For example, careful observation is one of the most important science tools. Observation means learning about things by using your senses. This includes taking in the whole picture as well as noticing the details.

Measuring

Measuring things helps you observe carefully and be certain your observations are correct. Scientists use measurements whenever possible in **investigations**. Sometimes what we think we observe is not accurate. Measuring helps us to see what is really there. For example, a full moon looks larger when it is near the **horizon**, the line where the sky meets the Earth. It seems smaller when it is high in the sky. But if you measure how wide it appears with a ruler held at arm's length at both heights, it comes out the same. Try it!

A magnifying glass can improve observation. It shows the detail in this fossil.

Look carefully at these rocks. What details do you observe? Write them down.

Improving observations

Other science tools simply help scientists make better observations. Microscopes, telescopes, measuring instruments, and tools such as video cameras extend scientists' ability to observe. For example, video cameras have even been strapped onto wild animals so we can see what they are looking at.

Scientists around the world use many high-tech tools. They use simple tools as well. Using tools as simple as a magnifying glass can improve observation. Van Leeuwenhoek started out with lenses that were only as strong as a hand-held magnifying lens.

TRY IT!

We do not always notice details. Have two people step out of the room. Then tell everyone who is left in the room to write down everything the missing people are wearing, including jewelry. Have them step back into the room. How accurate were everyone's observations?

Keeping good records

Taking good notes helps you see the results of an experiment clearly. It can help you review your work and help others understand your experiment. Real scientists record their results so that other scientists can repeat their experiments and see if they get the same findings. Only after an experiment is repeated with similar results do others accept the findings.

Van Leeuwenhoek lived long before cameras were invented. He drew pictures of the things he saw. He kept careful records describing the things he saw in detail. He also kept records of how he did his experiments. He wrote more than 500 letters to the Royal Society, a group of scientists in England. The society published many of the letters in its journal for other scientists to read.

Before cameras, scientists made careful drawings. These red-throated loons are by John James Audubon.

Scientists can even make notes underwater! This is useful when observing animals like the manatee.

Recording details

If you are doing an investigation, you should write down all of the steps in the scientific method. It is much better to record every little detail than to leave something out.

1. First write down a question you would like to answer. Record what you already know about it. Record any observations that relate to it. Take notes about any research you do.
2. Write down your hypothesis, or what you think is the answer. Include your reasons.
3. Next write down your plan for an experiment. Include a list of equipment you will need and describe how you will test your hypothesis.
4. Record how you conduct the experiment. Include your measurements. Anyone reading your records should understand what you did. They should be able to replicate (copy) your experiment exactly from your notes. Tell how you made it a **fair test** by keeping everything the same except for the one thing you tested (the **variable**).
5. Finally, record your conclusions. Based on the results of the experiment, was your hypothesis correct? What else did you learn? Would you like to experiment further or change the experiment? Communicate by showing your results in an easy-to-read form, such as a graph or chart.

Tools for Observing

Scientists use many tools that help them observe. Two of the most important tools in science have opened up new worlds—the telescope and microscope. Using the telescope, **astronomers** have been able to learn more about the Moon, planets, stars, and **galaxies**. Modern microscopes let us view the amazing microscopic world. Both of these tools use lenses to make things look larger, or magnify them.

Lenses

A lens is a piece of clear material that bends the light passing through it. The bending of light is called **refraction**. Light normally travels in a straight line. You may have observed a straight beam of light coming from a flashlight or car headlights. When rays of light hit the curved surface of a magnifying lens, their direction gets changed. They spread out. When those rays reach your eyes, the spread-out rays make objects look larger than they really are. They are magnified.

Lenses refract, or bend, light. Spread-out rays make a magnified image.

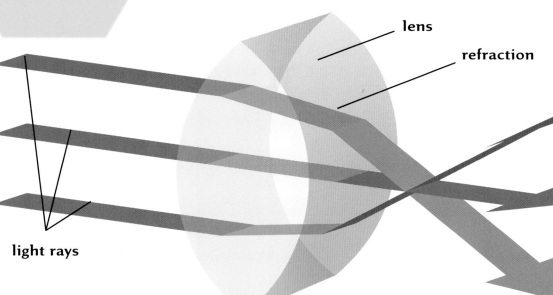

lens

refraction

light rays

A telescope uses two lenses to magnify distant objects twice. By using two lenses, things appear much larger than they would with just one lens. Some telescopes have curved mirrors instead of lenses. Mirrors can be larger than lenses and are used for more powerful telescopes.

A hand lens is a magnifying lens with a handle. You can use one to see small details such as the tiny crystals on a rock. Hold the lens about 5 inches (12 centimeters) in front of your eye. Then move the object under it until it is **focused**.

Use a magnifying lens to observe small objects or details.

TRY IT!

A glass of water is a lens. Hold one up near your face and look through it. Put your finger behind it and observe it through the glass. It is magnified because of refraction.

Microscopes

The most powerful microscopes are called **electron** microscopes. They can magnify objects up to several million times. Instead of using lenses to bend light, they fire a stream of electrons at the object to be viewed. The electrons form an image on a screen. Electron microscopes are expensive. They can help scientists see extremely small things such as **viruses**.

Microscopes in school

The microscopes used in school use light and lenses, not electrons. Two different lenses refract light coming from the viewed object. It gets magnified twice, so it appears much larger. Some microscopes use a mirror under the viewed object to shine light on it. Others have a built-in light.

This is a simple microscope, similar to the ones used in many schools.

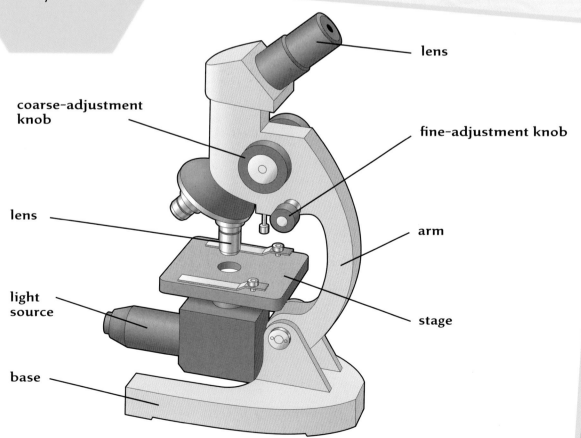

lens

coarse-adjustment knob

fine-adjustment knob

lens

arm

light source

stage

base

TRY IT!

Make your own microscope by putting a drop of water on a clear piece of plastic. Make some kind of a stand to hold the lens. Place objects under it and see how they are magnified.

How to use a microscope

1. When you use a microscope, never touch the lenses. If you carry a microscope, use two hands. Treat it gently.
2. The object you are looking at should be placed on a clear glass or plastic slide. Place it on the **stage** of the microscope, under the lens, after you have raised the eyepiece up as far as you can.
3. Use the lowest power lens first. If you have more than one lens on your microscope the lowest power lens is the shortest. Focus the slide by using the coarse-adjustment knob until it is almost clear. Then use the fine-adjustment knob.
4. Once your microscope is in focus, you can try the higher-power lenses. Turn the higher-power lens into place. Be sure the lens will not hit the slide! For these lenses you must use the fine-adjustment knob only.

Some microscopes do not have higher-power lenses. With these microscopes, you just put the object on a slide, put it on the stage, and focus.

lowest powered lens

middle powered lens

highest powered lens

Handle microscopes very gently.

13

Measurement

To find the amount of something by counting or comparing it to something else, you measure it. You could be counting heartbeats, dolphins, or galaxies. Or you could be finding how much something weighs, or how hot it is. When we measure time, length, **volume**, weight, or the temperature of things, we use standard measurements such as seconds, meters, liters, grams, or **degrees**. But you could measure using all kinds of different things—paper clips, for example.

Measurement in investigations

In the scientific method, numbers give a more accurate picture of what is going on. That is why the scientific method uses measurements. Other scientists can trust the results of an experiment that uses measurements. They can copy an experiment if they know the measurements. The **scientific community** only accepts the results of an experiment after it is successfully copied.

These containers each hold the same amount of liquid. Measurement is important because sometimes our eyes fool us.

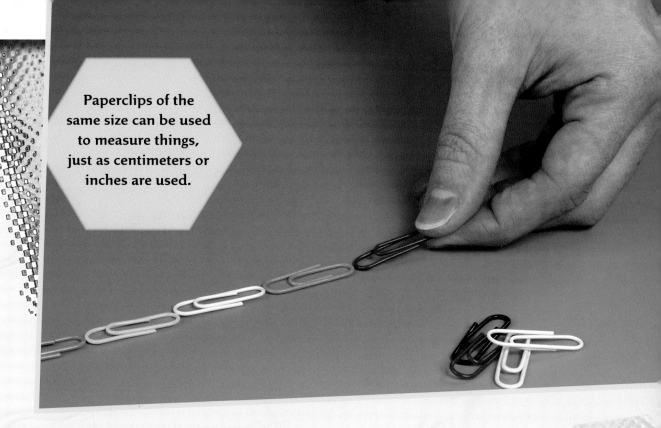

Paperclips of the same size can be used to measure things, just as centimeters or inches are used.

Standardized measurements

Using paper clips, try measuring the width and length of your desk and other objects. Should the paper clips all be the same size? Yes! If the whole class measures desks, should they all be using the same size clips? Yes! Why? Otherwise, the same-sized desk could vary in how many clips wide it is.

People realized centuries ago that we need **standardized** measurements (measurements that are all the same). Before that, one cup of water was whatever size of cup someone had. Now, a cup is an exact amount that everyone has agreed on.

DID YOU KNOW?

Hundreds of years ago, people used their bodies to measure things. A cubit was the length of a person's arm from elbow to middle-finger tip. An inch was the distance from the tip of the thumb to the first joint. The foot was, you guessed it, a foot. But parts of the body are not the same length for everyone, so this could cause problems.

The metric system

In the past, people in different places used many different systems to measure things. This led to problems. About 200 years ago, Napoleon Bonaparte was the ruler of France. People in different parts of France were using different systems of weights and measures. Napoleon decided that France needed a standardized system.

He asked scientists to come up with a system that made sense and was easy to work with. The system they developed is called the metric system. Most of the world uses it today. The modern form of the metric system is known as the Système International (International System), or the SI. It was adopted for worldwide use in 1960. Scientists everywhere use the metric system.

Units of length

Everything in the metric system is based on multiples of ten. The base unit for measuring length is the meter. A centimeter (meter with the **prefix** centi) is equal to 1/100 of a meter. Add the prefix milli, and you have a millimeter, 1/1,000 of a meter. Add kilo to meter, and you have a kilometer, 1000 × 1 meter or 1,000 meters.

Napoleon Bonaparte's metric system has helped scientists all over the world.

Units of mass

The base unit for measuring **mass** is the gram. Add the prefix *kilo* to the front, and you have a kilogram, equal to 1,000 grams. A gram's mass is about as much as that of a small paper clip. For measuring tiny things such as the amount of medicine in a pill, milligrams (1/1,000 of a gram) are used.

Units of volume

For liquid volume the liter is the base unit. A milliliter is 1/1,000 of a liter. Milliliters are tiny. It takes five of them to make one teaspoon.

A liter container is equal to a cube ten centimeters tall, ten centimeters wide, and ten centimeters deep. That equals 1,000 **cubic** centimeters. A milliliter is the same volume as one cubic centimeter (cm³.) A cubic centimeter is a cube one centimeter long, one centimeter wide, and one centimeter high. Solids are measured in cubic units, like cubic centimeters and cubic meters.

The metric system is easy to multiply and divide because it is based upon multiples of ten.

Length and Distance
10 millimeters (mm) = 1 centimeter (cm)
100 centimeters (cm) = 1 meter (m)
1,000 meters (m) = 1 kilometer (km)

Volume
1 cubic centimeter = 1 cm × 1 cm × 1 cm
1 cubic centimeter (cc or cm³) = 1 milliliter (mL)
1 liter (L) = 1,000 milliliters (mL)

Mass
1,000 milligrams (mg) = 1 gram (g)
1,000 grams (g) = 1 kilogram (kg)

Using Measuring Tools

Some experiments call for measuring length or distance. We can measure length with rulers, meter sticks, or tape measures. Be careful—some rulers have the zero at the end. Others have it near the end. The zero must be placed next to one end of the thing you are measuring. Read the ruler measurement next to the other end. Because scientists always use the metric system, even in the United States, you should too.

Measuring volume

Other experiments require volume measurements. Volume is the amount of space something takes up. In the metric system, liquids are measured in liters and milliliters. Solids are measured in cubic centimeters. To measure liquids, use **beakers**, flasks, measuring cups, or **graduated cylinders**.

You have probably used measuring cups in your kitchen. They can be used for experiments, but scientists usually use beakers instead. A beaker is similar to a measuring cup but has no handles. The glass ones used in labs can be heated. In school, they are sometimes made of plastic which cannot be heated.

This ruler shows both inches and centimeters.

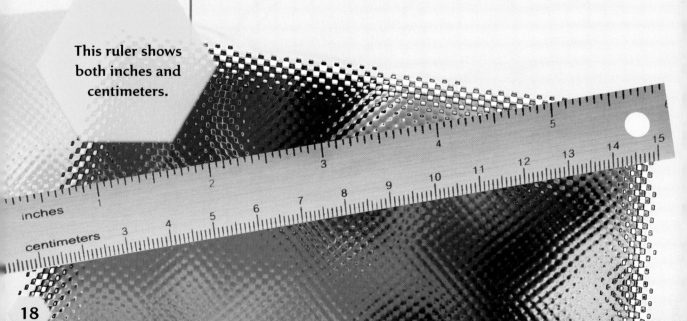

Measure the volume of a rock. Fill a beaker or measuring cup half full of water. Record the volume of the water in milliliters. Sink a rock in the water. Measure the water level again. Subtract the water-only level from the rock-and-water level. A cubic centimeter is the same volume as a milliliter. The number you end up with is the volume of the rock in cubic centimeters.

Graduated cylinders are tube-shaped containers marked with measurement lines. "Graduated" means the cylinder has marks for measurement. For small amounts the graduated cylinder is the most accurate tool for measuring liquids.

To use a graduated cylinder:

1. Put on safety goggles.
2. Place the container on a flat, level surface.
3. Turn it so the measurements face you.
4. Pour the liquid in carefully.
5. Read the measurement with your eyes level with the top of the liquid.

50 : 1
ml In 20°C
±1,0 ml 50

4

30

Find out which measuring equipment is used in your classroom.

Measuring mass and weight

In some experiments you must weigh things. In science books you may have noticed a weighed object is measured using "**mass**" instead of "weight." The mass of something is the amount of **matter** in it. Matter is anything that takes up space. Solids, liquids, and gases are matter. You are made of matter. To measure your matter, you step on a scale. If it reads 110 pounds (50 kilograms), that is your mass. Scientists say mass instead of weight because mass stays the same everywhere.

If you go to the Moon, your mass will still be the same. But weight depends on the pull of **gravity** on your mass. Earth's gravity is a force that pulls us toward it. Other things in space, such as the Moon, also have gravity. If you stepped on a scale on the Moon, you would weigh less. That is because the Moon's gravity is weaker than Earth's. It does not pull your body down onto the scale as hard as on Earth. There are places in space where you would be weightless. You could float. If you put your feet against a scale it would read close to zero. But you would still have the same mass.

On the Moon, astronauts weighed less. Their mass didn't change.

Even on Earth, your weight would be a tiny bit less on a high mountain than in a deep valley. Earth's gravity gets weaker the farther an object is from the center of the planet. Using mass instead of weight is a more accurate way of measuring something because the mass of an object stays the same in any location.

Balance scales

You can measure mass using a balance scale. Follow these steps to use a balance scale.

1. First, make sure the empty pans of the balance scale are balanced. A pointer on the base can show that they are even.
2. Place an object in one pan.
3. Add masses (weights) to the other pan until the two sides balance.
4. Add up the masses. The total is the mass of the object.

Here, a simple balance scale is used.

Measuring temperature

When you measure temperature you are measuring how hot or cold something is. A thermometer is a tool for measuring temperature. *Thermo* means "heat," and *meter* means "measure."

Liquids expand (spread out) when heated and contract (shrink) when cooled. Many years ago scientists realized they could put liquid in a tube and use it to measure temperature. As the liquid expands, it rises up the tube. When it contracts, it falls.

In 1742 Anders Celsius marked off degrees (units for measuring temperature) on one of these tubes. Water boils at 100 degrees Celsius (100°C) and freezes at 0 degrees Celsius (0°C). In science the Celsius scale is used throughout the world.

There are many experiments in which you would need to measure temperature. Some thermometers used today are **digital** and display numbers. But most school thermometers use a red-colored liquid or mercury. Mercury is a silver liquid that is dangerous if it is not contained in the thermometer.

Swedish scientist Anders Celsius provided an alternative to the Fahrenheit scale (°F).

Tips for using thermometers

1. If you are measuring the temperature of the air, make sure the thermometer is not in direct sunlight. It would throw off the measurement.

2. Read the measurement next to the top of the liquid. Sometimes each line represents one degree, sometimes two degrees or more. Make sure you know which scale your thermometer uses.

3. If you are measuring something that is being heated or cooled, take the temperature quickly. If you are measuring the temperature of something that is not being heated or cooled, let the thermometer sit for a couple of minutes before reading it.

4. If you are using a mercury thermometer (the liquid looks silver) and it breaks, do not touch the mercury. It is not safe. Ask your teacher for help.

This outdoor thermometer clearly shows the temperature in Celsius and Fahrenheit.

DID YOU KNOW? In the United States, scientists use the Celsius scale. However, the Fahrenheit scale is still used for weather reports and most other things in the United States.

Measuring time

Around 400 years ago, a famous scientist named Galileo Galilei was among the first people to see the need for careful experimenting. He understood the importance of measurements. He knew how important it would be for scientists to measure time accurately. In his lifetime there were clocks, but they were not reliable.

Galileo soon discovered that **pendulums** keep accurate time. A pendulum is a hanging weight that can swing freely back and forth. Galileo developed pendulum clocks for scientists to measure time in their experiments. Since then, better timepieces have been developed. Some can measure within a tiny fraction of a second.

This picture shows Galileo experimenting with a pendulum clock.

DID YOU KNOW?

Galileo was a scientific genius. He lived around 400 years ago. He was the first person to look into space using a telescope. Once, he watched a hanging lamp swing in a church. He used his **pulse** to time each swing. He learned that the swings kept a steady beat, even as they got smaller, until the lamp settled into place. He learned that pendulums keep a reliable beat. Later, he developed pendulum clocks.

Stopwatches

Many experiments need time measurements. You might need to know how long it takes an animal to run through a maze. You may need to know how long it takes an ice cube to melt, or a battery to run down. You may want to time heartbeats.

You can measure time with a clock or watch, but the best way is with a stopwatch. Digital stopwatches show you time with numbers. Analog stopwatches have hands that move around a clock dial.

Here is how to use a digital or analog stopwatch:

1. First set the watch to zero.
2. When you want to begin timing something, press start.
3. Press stop when you want it to stop.
4. Read the minutes, seconds, and fractions of a second on the display or dial.

Use either a digital (left) or analog (right) stopwatch for accurate timing.

Testing heart rates

It might feel like your heart is beating faster after you jog, but how can you prove it? You can use a stopwatch and the scientific method to test your theory.

1 ⬡ **Observe and ask questions**
After running to catch a bus it feels like your heart is pounding. Does you heart really beat faster after you jog? Do research to find out more about how your heart works.

2 ⬡ **Form a hypothesis**
State what you think is the answer to your question. Based on your research and observations, you may decide that your heart does beat faster after jogging.

3 ⬡ **Plan an experiment**
You decide to count the number of heartbeats per fifteen seconds after jogging, and compare them to the number of heartbeats per fifteen seconds when you are resting.

You will need to work with a partner. Make sure you know how to find each other's pulse. Have your partner tilt her or his head back a little. Find the windpipe bulging down the middle of the throat. Lightly press the tips of your pointer and middle fingers right next to the windpipe on one side in the middle of the neck. You should feel a pulse.

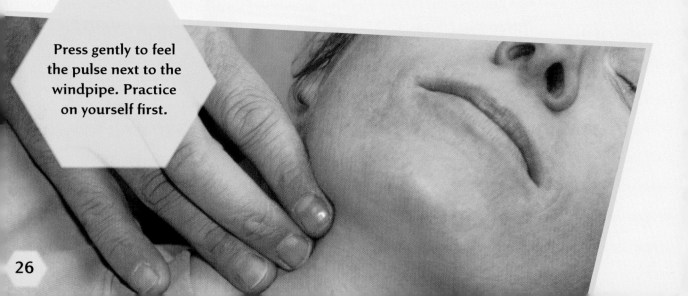

Press gently to feel the pulse next to the windpipe. Practice on yourself first.

The heart pumps blood around the body. The blood delivers food and oxygen to all parts of the body. Children have faster heart rates than adults. Babies' are even faster. In mammals, the smallest animals have the fastest heartbeats.

4 Conduct the experiment

First, time each other's resting pulse for fifteen seconds while sitting or lying down. Record your results. Do it again just to be sure you were accurate. Jog in place for three minutes and take the pulse again. Record the result and repeat again. If you are doing this in class, compile the results for the group.

5 Draw conclusions and communicate results

Show the results of the pulse rates in a chart or graph. Was your hypothesis proven or disproved by your results?

Do these results show that heart rates increased after jogging?

Number of heartbeats in 15 seconds, over two tests.

	Sitting 1	Sitting 2	Jogging 1	Jogging 2
Student 1	19	19	32	30
Student 2	28	26	31	33
Student 3	20	20	34	38
Student 4	22	23	35	30
Student 5	23	23	40	45

Using Models

Tools are not just for measuring. Sometimes scientists use models to help them do experiments. Models are also science tools. A model is a small representation of the real thing.

Scientists use models to study things that are too difficult to work with directly. Often, they use digital models on computers. In a science experiment, something that represents the real thing can be used as a model. In this experiment, a jar is used as a model of your foot.

This scientist holds an orange in one hand and a model of vitamin C (which is found in oranges) in the other.

1 **Observe and ask questions**
You have observed that clothes keep you warm by acting as insulators that trap your body heat. You wonder if wool socks keep your feet warmer than cotton socks. You learn all you can about wool and cotton.

2 **Form a hypothesis**
Your research leads you to say that wool socks will keep feet warmer. Now you need to test your hypothesis.

3 Plan an experiment

It would be difficult and possibly dangerous to wear a thermometer inside your socks. You decide to use a model instead—baby food jars filled with water. Your experiment uses eight jars, four wrapped in identical cotton socks and four in matching wool socks. You find cotton and wool socks all of the same thickness. You can measure the thickness by stacking them and using a ruler.

4 Conduct the experiment

All eight jars are filled with equal amounts of hot water from the same container at the same time. Thermometers are placed in the jars and the socks are wrapped around them quickly. All are wrapped the same. The jars are put on a tray. After five minutes, the thermometers are checked. Their temperatures are written down. The experiment is repeated.

5 Draw conclusions and communicate results

In all the jars wrapped in wool, the temperatures drop less. The wool is a better insulator. You show your results on a chart and write down all the details of your experiment.

In this test, jars are models for feet. This makes the experiment easy to control. Only the type of sock is variable.

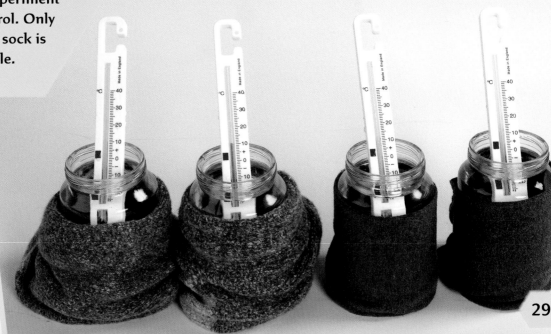

Putting It All Together

Making good observations will help you to understand how scientists work. Use microscopes, telescopes, or other tools to aid your observations. Make careful measurements and keep good records. Design experiments to test your hypotheses.

Observations, experiments, and measurements must mean something. You have to be able to **analyze** the information you get from them. Sometimes, students doing science investigations get confused by their experiments or come to conclusions that are not based on their results. Be careful. You have to know what your results mean.

Science helps us see and analyze faraway objects in space.

Use the scientific method

When you follow the steps of the scientific method, remember these things:

1. Observe and ask questions. Ask a clear science question you can answer with a straightforward, easy to understand experiment.
2. Form a hypothesis. Be precise. What do you think will happen? Don't make a wild guess.
3. Plan an experiment. Make sure your experiment really matches up with the hypothesis and answers your question clearly. Make it a fair test so only one thing can affect how it turns out.
4. Conduct the experiment. Measure, record, and repeat your experiment. Make sure to take careful notes.
5. Draw conclusions and communicate results. Make sure you do not jump to conclusions! Stick with what you have proven.

Of all the wonderful tools of science, the mind is the most important. The mind puts it all together.

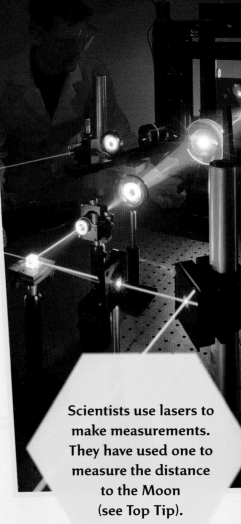

Scientists use lasers to make measurements. They have used one to measure the distance to the Moon (see Top Tip).

TOP TIP

The distance between the Earth and the Moon was measured accurately with an intense beam of light called a **laser**. The beam was bounced off of a reflector astronauts had left on the Moon's surface. Scientists measured the time it took for the beam to return to Earth. With their knowledge of the speed of light, they calculated the distance—just under 239,000 miles (385,000 kilometers). That is an example of how to put it all together!

Using computers

The computer is one of the greatest tools scientists have ever had. A computer carries out instructions. It takes in information. It processes that information. Then it gives out new information. Computers can take in lots of **data** and process it accurately at great speed. Work that would take years without a computer can be done in minutes.

A computer is a great analyzing tool. Scientists use computers to sort through and analyze large amounts of information gathered from experiments.

The Internet

The Internet has also become a powerful tool of science. The Internet has made it much easier for scientists to share information because it links computers together. Thousands of scientific articles and reports are published each year. Scientists can now read about the latest research in their field online. Then they can copy experiments or build on research they read about.

Computers are an important tool for all sorts of scientific investigation.

When van Leeuwenhoek discovered microbes in the 1600s, he wanted to tell other scientists about his discovery. He sent a letter to the Royal Society in England, describing what he had seen. They did not believe him. He kept writing to them. They finally sent people to see for themselves four years later. It would have been so much quicker if he could have emailed them a digital photo!

Students and computers

Computers and the Internet are great for students too. You can use computers to write reports. They can help you make graphs and charts. You can use a computer to get information and do research. Some websites let you submit questions for scientists or other experts to answer. There are instructions and ideas for science experiments online. If you want to learn more about or "do" science, the computer and the Internet are useful tools for you.

Students can use computers and the Internet for research.

Make Your Own Science Tools

You have learned how to use measuring tools but you can also make your own. Meteorology is weather science. Weather **satellites** provide much information to help forecast the weather. Local weather stations at ground level supply information to weather forecasters too.

Weather stations have instruments to measure temperature, air pressure, the moisture in the air, rainfall, wind, and other causes of weather. A rain gauge measures rainfall. Rainwater is measured in centimeters. You can make your own rain gauge.

How many centimeters of rain will fall during a heavy storm?

Materials
You will need:
- a ruler
- a can or jar that has straight sides. Your container must have a cylinder shape.

Steps
1. First, set the gauge where it will not tip over and where extra rain will not get splashed into it. Put it where leaves and other things are not likely to fall into it. Think of a way to keep it from being blown or knocked over.

2. After a rainfall, measure the depth of the water in the container. Put the zero end of a ruler into the water until it touches the bottom. Read the measurement at the surface.

3. Record the measurement. Then pour out the rainwater so you can measure the next rainfall. You can measure the rain from one rainfall or keep track of rain for as long as you like.

Read the measurement at the water line and make a record.

TRY IT!

Investigate to see if your rain measurements match the ones the newspaper or television gives. Make a hypothesis that says whether they will match or they will not. Plan your experiment. Do you want to measure rainfall for a day, a week, or a month? Keep records. Compare your results to weather reports. Draw your conclusion. Did your measurements match? Perhaps you will learn that rainfall can be quite different from place to place, even in the same city.

Measuring the Wind

The direction of the wind is important in predicting the weather. Wind often blows storms from one place to another. Winds are named for the direction from which they come. A west wind blows from the west. With a weather vane, the arrow points to the direction from which the wind is coming. So if it points north, a north wind is blowing. You can make a weather vane.

Weather vanes are often used as ornaments, but they are useful tools.

1 **Materials**

You will need:

- a piece of thin cardboard
- a plastic straw
- a pencil with an eraser on top
- a straight pin
- a paper cup
- modeling clay or sand

2 **Put it together**

1. First make the arrow. Cut a piece of cardboard into a triangle. Two sides should be about 4 inches (10 centimeters) long. The bottom should be about 2.4 inches (6 centimeters) long. Cut the tip off of your triangle, about 1 inch (3 centimeters) from the top. The cut should be parallel to the triangle's bottom. That tip will be your pointer. The rest is the tail.

Monsoons are seasonal winds. By studying with weather vanes and other devices, scientists know when the monsoons will occur, and from which direction they will blow.

2. Next cut a slit 1 inch (3 centimeters) long in the middle of one end of the straw. Slip the tail into the slit. In the other end, cut a shorter slit in the same direction. Insert the pointer. Make both ends line up straight. Cut new slits if you need to in order to get both ends to line up straight.

3. Then poke a pin through the middle of the straw into the eraser. The pointer should be balanced and able to swing in all directions. Make adjustments if needed.

4. Finally, make a stand for your vane. Cover a ball of modeling clay with a paper cup and poke the pencil through the cup base, into the clay. Alternatively, fill a cup with sand and push the pencil into it. Make sure the pencil is held upright.

5. Take your weather vane outside. Use a compass to tell you the directions. Mark them on the container.

Make sure the pencil is held firm, so that only the pointer moves in the wind outside.

Make an anemometer

An **anemometer** is a tool for measuring how fast the wind blows. Here is a simple way to make one.

1 **Materials**
You will need:
- four paper cups
- a heavy paper plate or a disposable plastic one
- a nail or a long pin
- a long, thin stick, such as a meter stick
- a stapler

2 **Put it together**
1. First mark or color one cup so it looks different from the others. Measure to find the exact center of the plate. Then poke a hole there.
2. Next staple the cups to the edge of the plate. They must be spaced evenly around the plate. If the plate were a clock, they would be at 12:00, 3:00, 6:00, and 9:00.
3. Make sure the top of each cup faces the bottom of the one next to it. That way as the anemometer spins, the cups will face the same direction when they reach 12:00.

4. Insert the pin or hammer the nail through the hole and then into the stick. The plate must be loose enough to spin. Finally, hammer the stick into the ground in a windy spot.

5. Watch the cups turn in the wind. Count the number of turns the marked cup makes in a minute. The larger the number, the faster the wind.

This anemometer can provide you with very simple measurements of wind speed.

DID YOU KNOW?

The Beaufort Wind Scale is used to describe wind strength using the effect of wind on things in its path.

Force 0   Calm, no wind. Smoke rises straight up.

Force 1–3   Light wind, flags blow out.

Force 4–5   Moderate wind. Small trees sway. Lakes have waves.

Force 6–7   Strong wind. Walking is hard and large trees sway.

Force 8–9   Gale. Shingles blow off roofs.

Force 10–11   Storm. Buildings are damaged.

Force 12   Hurricane. Severe damage to property.

Science Safety

Real scientists take care to stay safe when they are doing investigations. You should too. Use protective gloves, safety glasses, and other protective gear when necessary.

If you use science equipment, always be careful. Use equipment and materials appropriately. That way they will not be damaged and neither will you. Microscopes, lenses, thermometers, scales, and other equipment are costly and can be damaged or destroyed if not used carefully. Always behave responsibly with them.

Safety at home

You may want to do scientific experiments at home. Make sure an adult knows what you are doing. Never play around with electricity from an outlet. Use stoves or other heat sources with permission only. Some household chemicals are dangerous. Use them only with supervision.

Safety glasses can protect your eyes from glass and chemicals.

Scientists take safety very seriously. They wear protective clothing and handle equipment carefully.

Safety at school

In class, follow instructions for using materials. Ask your teacher if you are not sure what to do. Never put things in your mouth unless instructed to. Use safety goggles to protect your eyes if the activity calls for them. Any equipment that is made of glass must be handled with great care. If glass gets broken, ask an adult to help pick it up. Do not get cut!

Clean up after yourself. Keep things tidy. Scientists keep things orderly. Put everything back in its proper place. Wash your hands when you are done. Be careful not to touch chemicals or other things that may be harmful.

If you spill something, tell the teacher. Wipe it up immediately, unless it is something dangerous. Report any accident or injury right away to your teacher or another adult.

TOP TIP

Follow safety guidelines in class when doing investigations. When in doubt, ask a teacher or other adult. Most accidents can be prevented. Fooling around and not following directions can mess up experiments and sometimes cause harm.

Being a Scientist

If you want to learn how to be a scientist, use science tools. Careful observation is an excellent tool for learning about the world. Use your eyes and other senses.

Other tools help scientists observe things too. Microscopes, telescopes, and thousands of other scientific instruments take our eyes and minds to places they could not go without them.

Measurement

Scientists use the metric system and tools such as thermometers, stopwatches, metric rulers, graduated cylinders, and balance scales. Measurements make the results of experiments clear. They keep our eyes and opinions from tricking us. Models are tools for doing experiments when using the real thing would be difficult or impossible.

Telescopes allow us to observe other worlds.

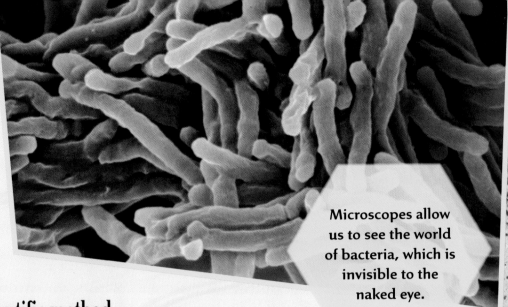

Microscopes allow us to see the world of bacteria, which is invisible to the naked eye.

The scientific method

The scientific method is one of the greatest tools of science. It is a careful, orderly, and exact way to learn about the world. Scientists ask questions and do careful experiments to find the answers. They share their findings with others.

Keeping good records is an important part of the method. Scientists use records to communicate their results to others. Records help scientists understand investigations.

Computers and the Internet

Computers are tools that scientists use in many ways. They help analyze information. They are useful in experiments. Both computers and the Internet are used in research and in communicating with other scientists. Both are speeding up the progress of science.

How to be a scientist

We can all use science to learn about the world. If you like science, you might work in a scientific field someday. But even if you do not enjoy science you can use some of the tools of science in your work. Until then, keep learning about science. It has a strong impact on the world in which we live. The more you learn about scientific achievements and discoveries, the more you will be amazed. Stay curious, ask questions, observe, and test things out. But remember that safety comes first. That is how to be a scientist.

The Metric System

SI MEASURES (METRIC)

Temperature
0 degrees Celsius (°C): water freezes
100 degrees Celsius (°C): water boils

Length and Distance
10 millimeters (mm) = 1 centimeter (cm)
100 centimeters (cm) = 1 meter (m)
1,000 meters (m) = 1 kilometer (km)

Volume
1 cubic centimeter = 1 cm × 1 cm × 1 cm
1 cubic centimeter (cc or cm³) = 1 milliliter (mL)
1,000 milliliters (mL) = 1 liter (L)

Mass
1,000 milligrams (mg) = 1 gram (g)
1,000 grams (g) = 1 kilogram (kg)
1,000 kilograms (kg) = 1 metric ton

CUSTOMARY MEASURES (SOMETIMES CALLED IMPERIAL)

Temperature
32 degrees Fahrenheit (°F): water freezes
212 degrees Fahrenheit (°F): water boils

Length and Distance
12 inches (in) = 1 foot (ft)
3 feet (ft) = 1 yard (yd)
5,280 feet (ft) = 1 mile (mi)

Volume of liquids
8 fluid ounces (fl oz) = 1 cup (c)
2 cups (c) = 1 pint (pt)
2 pints (pt) = 1 quart (qt)
4 quarts (qt) = 1 gallon (gal)

Weight
16 ounces (oz) = 1 pound (lb)
2,000 pounds (lb) = 1 ton (T)

CONVERTING METRIC MEASURES TO CUSTOMARY MEASURES

Temperature

0 degrees Celsius (°C) = 32 degrees Fahrenheit (°F)	0 degrees Fahrenheit (°F) = -18 degrees Celsius (°C)
100 degrees Celsius (°C) = 212 degrees Fahrenheit (°F)	100 degrees Fahenheit (°F) = 38 degrees Celsius (°C)

To convert degrees Fahrenheit to degrees Celsius, subtract 32, then multiply the result by 5 and divide by 9. For example, if it is 80 degrees Fahrenheit, it is 26.7 degrees Celsius:

80 - 32 = 48
48 × 5 = 240
240/9 = 26.7

To convert degrees Celsius to degrees Fahrenheit, simply reverse the process. Multiply by 9, divide by 5, and add 32. For example, if it is 20 degrees Celsius, it is 68 degrees Fahrenheit:

20 × 9 = 180
180/5 = 36
36 + 32 = 68

Length and Distance

1 centimeter (cm) = 0.394 inches (in)	1 inch (in) = 2.54 centimeters (cm)
1 centimeter (cm) = 0.032 feet (ft)	1 foot (ft) = 30.48 centimeters (cm)
1 meter (m) = 39.37 inches (in)	1 inch (in) = 0.025 meters (m)
1 meter (m) = 3.28 feet (ft)	1 foot (ft) = 0.305 meters (m)
1 kilometer (km) = 3280 feet (ft)	1 foot (ft) = 0.0003 kilometer (km)
1 kilometer (km) = 0.621 miles (mi)	1 mile (mi) = 1.609 kilometers (km)

Volume

1 milliliter (mL) = 0.034 fluid ounces (fl oz)	1 fluid ounce (fl oz) = 29.57 milliliters (mL)
1 milliliter (mL) = 0.002 pint (pt)	1 pint (pt) = 473 milliliters (mL)
1 liter (L) = 33.81 fluid ounces (fl oz)	1 fluid ounce (fl oz) = 0.029 liters (L)
1 liter (L) = 2.113 pints (pt)	1 pint (pt) = 0.473 liters (L)

Mass/Weight

1 gram (g) = 0.035 ounces (oz)	1 ounce (oz) = 28.35 grams (g)
1 kilogram (kg) = 35.27 ounces (oz)	1 ounce (oz) = 0.028 kilogram (kg)
1 kilogram (kg) = 2.20 pounds (lb)	1 pound (lb) = 0.454 kilogram (kg)
1 metric ton = 2,205 pounds (lb)	1 pound (lb) = 0.0005 metric ton
1 metric ton = 1.102 tons (T)	1 ton (T) = 0.907 metric ton

Glossary

analyze to see how the pieces fit together and to make sense of information

anemometer instrument used to measure wind speed

astronomer person who studies planets, stars, moons, and other things in space

bacteria one-celled living things that can only be seen through a microscope

beaker glass or plastic cup with a pouring lip and no handle

cubic shaped like a cube, as in cubic centimeter

data information

degree unit used to measure temperature

digital storing or expressing information as a string of numbers

electron tiny particle

fair test changing one thing at a time in an experiment while keeping everything else the same

focused made clear, not blurry

galaxy very large group of stars

graduated cylinder tube-shaped container marked with lines for measuring liquids or solids

gravity force that attracts an object toward the center of Earth

horizon line where the sky appears to meet land

hypothesis (more than one are called hypotheses) answer to a question that can be tested by doing an experiment

investigation using the scientific method to learn something

laser intense beam of light

lens piece of clear material curved on one or both sides to bend light passing through it

mass amount of liquid, gas, and solid in an object

matter anything that has weight and takes up space

microscope device that makes tiny things look larger, usually by using lenses

observation learning with the senses, especially by seeing

pendulum hanging weight that can swing freely back and forth

prefix one or more letters attached to the front of a base word to form a new word

pulse beat of blood through the body caused by the beating of the heart

refraction bending of light

satellite object that circles around Earth in space

scientific community all the world's scientists

scientific method scientific way of finding things out, usually following these steps: observation, asking questions, forming a hypothesis, planning and conducting experiments, drawing conclusions, and sharing results

stage part of a microscope where a slide is placed for viewing

standardized all made the same

variable something that can be changed in an experiment

virus extremely tiny thing that can cause disease

volume amount of space that something takes up, measured in cubic units or liquid measurements such as milliliter and liter

Further Reading

Goldsmith, Mike. *Galileo Galilei*. Chicago: Raintree, 2002

Jones, Lorraine. *Super Science Projects about Weather and Natural Forces*. New York: Rosen Publishing, 2000

Rodgers, Alan, and Angella Streluk. *Temperature*. Chicago: Heinemann Library, 2002

Rogers, Kirsteen. *The Usborne Complete Book of the Microscope*. Tulsa, OK: EDC Publishing, 1999

Index